Too Blue for Logic

MARIANNE JONES

Published by Cinnamon Press
Meirion House
Glan yr afon
Tanygrisiau
Blaenau Ffestiniog
Gwynedd
LL41 3SU
www.cinnamonpress.com

The right of Marianne Jones to be identified as author of this work has been asserted by her in accordance with the Copyright, Designs and Patent Act, 1988. Copyright © 2009 Marianne Jones
ISBN: 978-1-905614-70-7
British Library Cataloguing in Publication Data. A CIP record for this book can be obtained from the British Library.

Designed and typeset in Palatino by Cinnamon Press. Cover design by Mike Fortune-Wood from original artwork 'blue cornflower in water' by Elen, agency: dreamstime.com.
Printed by the MPG Books Group in the UK

The publisher acknowledges the financial assistance of the Welsh Books Council

Acknowledgments

I would like to thank the editors of the following magazines and books in which several of the poems in this volume first appeared: *The New Welsh Review, Coffee House Poetry, Borderlines, MsLexia, Red Poets, Kindred Spirits Quarterly, An Anglesey Anthology* (Gwasg Carreg Gwalch), *In Love* (Leaf Books), *The Lie of the Land* (Cinnamon Press), *Mint Sauce* (Cinnamon Press).

Special thanks to my dynamic, super-efficient editor, Jan Fortune-Wood, and to the poet, Nessa O'Mahony, for her detailed reading of the text. Thank you to the following poets for helpful comments on poems: Fiona Owen, Mike Thomas, Carol Ann Duffy, Gillian Clarke, Manon Ceridwen, John Fraser Williams. I would also like to thank my family and friends for all their encouragement and, in particular, my husband, Gerry Wolff.

Biblical quotations (see notes) are taken from The New Revised Standard Version (Anglicized Edition), copyright 1989, 1995 by the Division of Christian Education of the National Council of the Churches of Christ in the United States of America. Used by permission. All rights reserved.
The epigraph to 'Soul', 'You sod,/leave my soul alone' is from 'In the theatre' by Dannie Abse, *New and Collected Poems* (Hutchinson, 2003), © Dannie Abse 2003, used by kind permission of the author.

Notes

Soul: *Satori* means 'enlightenment' (Japanese)
Hallowe'en: *Tatami* are mats made of rice straw used on Japanese floors and *kanji* are Chinese characters, also used in Japanese script. The 'second angel' is an allusion to The Revelation of St. John the Divine (Rev.8:8) & 'blessed are the merciful' is from the Sermon on the Mount, Matthew 5:7. Extracts from both are read at the Mass for All Saints on November 1st. 'Mystical rose' is from the Litany of the Blessed Virgin.
Momiji: momiji are coloured autumn leaves (Japanese).

Contents

for Gerry
and for my mother and father

Too Blue for Logic

New Year

The temple bell
resonates across the snow.
Midnight—time to begin afresh.
I pull the oil heater closer,
notice your sideways glance.

A young wife has no power here.
What need of that with love?
It is a silly statement in a book.
What do I know of mother-in-laws,
of plots in another room?

Later, I learn that war
casts years of shadow over peace
and turn to Zen
so even the ridge tiles of a shrine,
light shining through a porcelain cup,
shores up my crumbling faith.

Confession

In the contemporary church,
with chairs in a circle
round the altar,
the priest says cheerfully
that I must stay.

I tell him about the night
you poisoned me. He does not believe,
sweeps it aside with one hand,
warns me of excommunication
if I leave.

Outside, the wind blows grit
into my eyes. My feet are iron,
hard to lift. I stop
beside a flower stall to catch my breath
and drink in colour.

Tokyo Train

A man's goldfish mouth opens.
His eyes stare through fishbowl lenses.
Others gaze without sight
as if they've tasted Lethe water.

This dwarf star carriage
crushes each atom.

> I feel you stand in the shadow
> clutching your phial of poison.

Windows are my salvation.
Through them I see camellia
flower in snow, or now
the macramé of streets
with knots of shops around stations
and among highrise, lowrise concrete
a slick of land, survivor,
with tanks of red and orange carp.

Soul

'You sod,
leave my soul alone'
                    from In the theatre *by Dannie Abse*

Draw Tokyo at twilight
on a quiet street,
a lull in the day,
a child's song crackling
over loudspeakers
implying that it's time to go home.

There's no space to run
through the wind here
but I find a square yard of concrete,
skip and stop in cool air
to go upstairs.

Draw the blank white walls
of the unheated hostel
where once I opened
a door to a room
and time stopped.
Death became an illusion.
Satori, they said.

                    *

Sensitivity of the temporal lobes,
the surgeon on a *Radio 4*
discussion panel says.
I could perform a Godectomy
if anyone wanted it—
            and a songectomy,
            a speechectomy?

12

*

Draw me a Tokyo bathroom.
It's an oasis, the only safe room
because of a bar to bolt the door.

I'm sitting on the wooden slats
on top of a bath.
Gongs, beads, and the peal of bells,
all that elaborate language,
I leave for silence,
to pray for a Zen monk who is dying
but beyond the door, threats,
as my husband screeches abuse.

*You can slip poison into my food,
roll bottled gas towards me,
malign me, foil my attempts to escape,
but you will never touch my soul.*

*

Draw Tokyo at twilight
the end of an ordinary day,
a child's song crackling
over loudspeakers,
when time stops.

Hallowe'en

On All Souls' Eve,
the clocks gone back,
the land inked in blacks and greys,
jets destroy
the lyrical chattering of birds
as they scream towards
a blood-sodden sunset.

Where children collect blue mussel,
scallop shells, whelks,
they veer towards soft hills
and you cannot call them back
to land near Cymeran sands.
You cannot call the men
back to the safety of village lights.

*

I am not ashes to ashes
but heavy clay buttoned in clay
unable to move, to raise a hand,
except that the second angel
begins to chant the Sermon on the Mount—
blessed are the merciful

*

It was not winter, no,
but a summer's night,
the window wide
to let in the breeze,
but corners of the room
were Hallowe'en shadows
and whispers scraped like withered leaves
across the *tatami*.

There was a light in the centre.
They pushed me beneath it,
bided their time.

Their head, who raped Chinese girls
during the war,
ordered this meeting.

Filthy foreigner—
for fleeing from a husband
who fed me poison
and held a razor blade to my eyes.

You, whom I trusted once—
husband,
sadist, adulterer,
you sit black-suited, back upright,
a *kanji* for respectability.

I hear the wind in the pine trees.
I hear *rape her until she is silent.*
The men circle.

But the breeze, the window,
don't jump from floors below,
footsteps, door flung open,
run, world still there,
mystical rose.

Asthma

Yes, I met you before.
You made me a nun,
weighing the worth
of every word.

But tonight you steal in
like a bailiff
ready to disconnect my breath
as if I haven't paid my dues.

Whinnying of lungs
reined hard,
galloping heart
on some steep margin—

know
there is
nothing
to hold

pray
life
on earth
survives.

Near dawn
my island home whispers,
breathe like waves.

Daytime, unreal,
I walk with the footprints of a cloud
in a field full of yellow flowers.

House in the East

This house protects me.
My tending this house
comes back to me as a gift.

In its wood and *tatami*
is a mellow silence
that reaches beyond you.

Every room helps me escape
your raised hand. Each cup or book
brings me something deeper.

Every touch of its walls is known to me,
every light and shadow of passing days,
every dream that love will win out in the end.

The lily I put near the entrance
still lights up a corner
like a blessing.

And when I open the door to leave,
to first light and the pine tree's shadow,
I know, in whatever future,
this house protects me.

Change

When I came back
there was frost on the road
but I held the first snowdrop,
a star on my brow.

In my parents' window
the light was out.
My friends' laughter
teased behind hedges—
I chased
and found the shadowed snow.

This is my home, I cried.
It echoed on the night.
This is my island home.

I scanned the landscape
like a foreign language
and found a noun I knew,
a farm upon a hill,
embedded in an alien syntax.

Ynys Môn

The new road's fast.
turning you into a fragment
of low-lying land
on the way, in the way,
to Somewhere,
even though bluebells in the dingle,
summer on the beach and heather on Bodafon
spill like glass marbles
out of your woollen pocket.

Bryn Celli Ddu

The woman in shorts and cagoule
reads from a guide-book with no real answers.
We stare at worn patterns on stone.

Bones were found—broken backbone and skull
near the farm with the hens in the hay and the tractor rust.
On this morning of mirror glare from rain
aching to fall from the sky, we try to imagine.

The mountains are vague and grey.
They do not speak to us either. They keep their distance
or ask dull questions. The woman reads
about religious beliefs. Did their gods
demand human blood? Would they recognise us?

The Priest

Once
    I raised sacred
over ordinary streets.
    In my hands
I showed it.

Words, the *shibboleths* of centuries,
cannot describe it.
Maniples and chasubles,
crimson for fire and blood,
purple for penitence,
become a sideshow
next to this dark and shimmering
place of angels.

Music comes closer.
My congregation sings
Ave Maria to the thin air.

Of course, I realise
God doesn't sit on a chair
in the sky, patriarch in braces
with a gold fob, or tribal king,
but we are here by chance
and so I hesitate beside the door,
look up at the vacant stars.

And yet I hear the angels sing.

The James Dean Star

It threw a nuclear light on the lawn
as I sat in my car in the shadow of trees.

Think you will live forever, it carped,
awareness supported by kidneys and bone?
I mumbled words like birdsong, dawn.

What do I know of that? it scoffed,
a weariness across its face,
just like James Dean having a smoke.
From the first handprint to these garden trees,
from the first bacterium—just the beat of a wing.
Life is a layer thinner than skin.

*

Flo under the dryer
with the blue rinse perm
says, *Are you Pisces,*
the swimmer, the dreamer?

Your Fate in the stars:
should we drift with the tide
like dead sardines in a chemical spill
or put our handprints on the rock?

*

There used to be six rivers here
but they dried up during the drought.
Look—a lake shape, eroding gullies,
a whirlwind of dust coming ever closer,
turning the noon sky red.

Life is a layer thinner than skin
on this, the garden of Eden planet.

A drift of rain
and plants bloom in the desert, I said,
but my star was gone.

Searching for a House of the Soul

As it grows, the hermit crab has to leave its shell
and search for a larger one to live in.

Morning on the estate
in the plunge pool of routine
won't fit anymore, so I drive
mile after mile, searching.

Maybe it's here, on a canopied lane
where speedwell and red campions grow
and horsechestnuts unfurl leaves.

But the farm where we once,
somersault giggly with childhood,
drank unpasteurised milk
is now *hol. accom. cottage to let.*

Still, I can sit on the beach,
take off trainers and socks,
wiggle my toes, to find lid of pie,
lean pieces in rich gravy,
and an empty crisp bag.

Still from a grey-blue jug of sky
the sun pours out.
Boys tarzan in waves.
Mosquito jetski nags,
snags on morning.

The incoming sea licks
my complaining toes
like a wet dog. The wind freshens,
jippier, throws spray against Swnt island,
jibe-ho's me out of the ruts of thought.

A rucksack hoist on my back,
I flee to a café
to lean on cobalt blue oilcloth—
around me, teapot, sachets of sugar,
silk flowers in a sherry glass—
outside, the rain.

New World

You jive highwire on night,
fruit bloom city. A jazz of green, red,
voices, cars, cross your bridge
over reflections.

Lemon and lime fizz
in your café windows.
All your street lamps
exhale haloes
like dubious angels.

People tumble out of discos,
stumble home.
The colour bleaches from you
until first light
bruises your pavements,
reveals the wings
of scavenger seagulls.

This is a time to arrive
with an old suitcase in my hand,
a clenched address in my pocket,
an unknown grid of roads before me.

Canadian Journey

for my Canadian friends

Darkness:
I catch the glint of its eyes,
stars, scorching blue
the side of the train.

We're running past unseen lakes,
prairies, a fox by the tracks.
Perhaps we'll see northern lights.
Breath fogs the windows.

The repetition of wheels on rails
leads into trance.
I see the trail where I put
one snowshoe in front of another
in a land of bears.

It led towards us
skating with sparklers
on the Ottawa canal
and skiing down a mountain singing.

Someone opens a window,
lets in the vastness of the forest.

Arrival

I cycle, glancing over hedges,
on my way to Fishbourne
to see the mosaic.

It's boxed away, so I return
past spindly trees, down the A27,
past Bosham—no, turn
to go once more down country lanes
and find the church with Canute's daughter
buried in the vault, the sea
still rolling in.

I buy a toy for a new niece
and a hat made of Jacob's wool
to pull over my ears—the wind's sharp.

Alone at twilight
with the watercolour sky,
the lanes, my bike—
shipped over the Atlantic
for one Canadian dollar. I'm home.

After the War

Most days, you know the bedtime truce,
the warm milk, repeated *Red Riding Hood.*

You see her unravel a too-small sweater
for wool to knit you something new

and save each piece of string, paper,
second-hand hats—just in case.

And even though he can't come home,
in the garden, his apple trees stand guard,

with a battalion of cabbages,
to fight starvation.

Great Aunt

When I crossed the bridge,
I knew you stood there—
a rowan in summer
and glowing like your polished
copper kettle.

        I realized they were wrong in school:
        knowledge isn't acquired in straight lines.
        It is the seeing of a half-hidden shell.

There I was, gabardined again,
head down, going to church
to hear another sermon on BLEAK.

I was going to take the path
past the row of bitten houses,
across the cobbles,
into despair with the cross on top,
when I risked the anger,
took the other way,
and ran every step towards your home.

Island: Searching for a Language

1

In the beginning, saints
searched for the Word in sunrise
and in the Pentecostal flames of Autumn.

2

Shouts clarify its misty sky
as we, marble-rattling children,
break pond ice to taste coldness
and save birds.

On our estate,
the man next door comes home
carrying a brace of rabbits on his back
or, shouting wildly in the dark,
slurs into dustbins—
place of cabbage and tension,
hopscotch and quarrels,
near woods full of bluebells and steam trains
going up to the Pandy
where my Nain walks miles
for yoghurt or news.

Post-war babies—
on Thursdays we gull
round canteen windows
for lumps of cheese
under rationed sun:

                one egg a week
                2 oz of butter
                prefabs
                icy lino
                frost flowers on January windows.

3

What has this world to do
with sitting in the tower of Sneyd Hall
discussing the ambiguity of a poem?

Cut off from my people
                    who plough fields
                    sing hymns
                    do not pose
                    never say,
                    Bird thou never wert.

Can a poem be as honest
as ploughing a field
or the words ring so true
they stay with the warmth
of reworked wool next to your skin
and holes in your shoes
where the rain comes in?
Discuss.

4

Cut off, they said,
not by the sword
but by a blue-eyed Capulet girl,
a river of English and spark of Irish,
who fell in love with my Welsh Montague father.

What does this matter on a world scale—
these windblown islands of Britain?

I am unsure of the words
I heard in rhythms
from the room downstairs.

5

Can I tell in my words that you lived,
that you stood there in your March garden
throwing grain to a few hens?
Penny on the railway, you sang, Nain,
from a song about how to get to heaven.
What a relief to a Catholic child!
You'd give that to save me from hell,
wouldn't you?

6

Today we wander the island,
pass by Trefignath Stone Age cairn,
once large in the landscape, now reduced
by the metamorphosing language
of traffic and aluminium plant.

We hear the hymn of drills,
JCBs, trucks—
a tone-deaf choir
extolling the Bible of progress,
ploughing an expressway
past the barns of the superstores.

There is still a huddle of hazel,
hawthorn and small birds,
at the edge of this fenced field.

There is still a sky, a sun,
the quartzite of Holyhead mountain
and the sea
in this helicopter morning.

7

Nearby, in the ex-convent Art Centre,
I can still smell prayer exhaust
among children's paintings,
still spell with incense and candles
and see Jacob's ladder stretch upwards
past stained-glass windows and out of my reach.

This is no longer my language.
But when we leave,
I find the nouns of hills,
the verbs of moonrise and sunset,
the intonation of the sea.

Boat

Once we were lambs on a chalk hill,
a single rose in a mystical room.
You could sail goose-winged over the water,
glide into harbour with the swans.
My blinkered mind opened to colours
freshened as if after the rain.

Now the bridge has girders of ice.
The lines of current in the water
form thin floes. Our boat, clinker-built,
battles against an undertow,
flounders into a sandbank, fails.

What does it matter on a sunny morning
with strong coffee and the Sunday papers?
Every day, I look out over the sea.

In a Cafe

I slip away
on an old folk song,
a boat
rising and falling on waves,
leaving you
further and further behind
until I cannot see you
through the mist
that shrouds these northern islands,
cannot recall your lips,
your blue-green eyes.

A Lie

tonight
muslin air
shrouds the garden

even the flame
of orange tulip
greys

this is how our friendship
ended

not with cut knees
or the crack of marbles
on concrete

but with the suffocation
of mist

The Beach in Late Winter

A spring tide with froth like yeast
highjumps the wall,
leavens a bleached-out time of year:
the *coaches welcome* Wendon cafe closed,
the ice-cream booth shut until Easter,
and on the front, three empty benches.

I'm walking, frozen to a consonant,
a leaning forwards *r* pulling towards
a lane sheltered by hawthorn,
and catching glimpses of catkins,
finches flying inside a quarry,
a green buoy far out to sea.

Sunlight reminds me there are signs of change—
buds, shoots and nearly daffodils.

Untangled

Men at the door
try to sell me
double-glazing or Jehovah.

I start to write
but stare at mountains.
That lawnmower is loud—
I need a coffee.

It's tastier in anticipation.
I should clear my desk, my life.
It's *Feng Shui* or something.

But then the moon does it for me,
music out of noise,
rising in an azurine sky.

Grasshopper

Jade drop on harp-string legs,
feeling through fine hairs
the rough of cloth,
the smooth of glass,

you stumble into a place
of munching carrot and beetroot cake
as a big mammal booms,
What is a poem?

Here you pause,
pull up a suckered foot
to wash, and whisper,
I am a poem.

A Love Poem

for Gerry

On the way home from the hospital
the night before your operation,
I scratched the side of my car,
smashed the wing mirror,
drove round and round the ring road,
lost.

I don't remember what I thought about.
I didn't think
as tower blocks went past my windows again.
All I recalled was your good-natured face
and the word, *brainstem*.

In the morning, the staff called you
Hannibal the Cannibal
as they fastened you into a head frame
and played you Mozart.

I waited in the comfort of a park.
Beds of begonias
tried to spell out something
in their pink and yellow script,

but I couldn't read it,
not until later,
when you sat up
and asked for soup.

Too Blue for Logic

My axioms were so clean-hewn,
the joins of *thus* and *therefore* neat
but, I admit
life would not fit
between straight lines
and all the cornflowers said was *blue*,
all summer long, so blue.
So when the sea came in and with one wave
threatened to wash my edifice away,
I let it.

Memento Vita

The island's full
of images of woman—
madonna, maiden, mother
and in the garden
where bamboos whisper,
there's a statue of a girl skipping,
her future stretching before her
down an avenue of flowers.

Lost

And you can run through endless mazes
down the alley by the side of a canal
into a dead end with yellow stucco,
peeling poster, geranium on a ledge,
washing high up.
             You backtrack,
sweat to find that chink
that leads into the blaze of square
with tables, waiters, striped umbrellas,
but still feel trapped within some plot:
that man glances quick, bright,
hides behind a dark moustache;
in a corner, they plan, among pigeons,
an assignation, or deep into alchemy
drink espresso and scheme—
but you are caught by glass,
ornate facades, Vivaldi's music.

At night, the players take the stage
in beaded costumes, purple, black,
and stare out from under masks.

Summer Garden

His ashes were scattered here.
No trace of a presence remains—
just the scent of bark
and flap of a blackbird's wing
as it eases from heat
into a canopy of leaves.

A man with big-boned paces
marches through
intent on somewhere else.

A jet, stiff as a rusted hinge,
warps Sussex out of rural
then releases it
back into Wolds,
back to a butterfly
dancing round tall roses.

Nectarine

Foreigner, your red coat
with jagged yellow splash
and purple flush
bruises, though juice springs from you
like laughter and you roll summer
into a smooth-skinned ball.
At your centre, you keep your self,
all your ancestors,
all your descendants, an orchard,
in wood-stone stillness.

Raspberries

In May, you sit in prim and sour rows,
your bodies tight pixels of green,
children in church
warned of the sin of ripening:

look at that hussy dribble-juice
sucked to death by flies
with glinting metallic backs;
look at those fallen into the ditch and trampled
because the Lord was not well pleased.

But in July, when the sun
sits on the shoulder of heaven,
you blush into sweetness.

The Beach in Late Summer

Clouds bubble up in the after-harvest air.
Oiled sunbathers, colonies of seals
on sand, sleep on.

Evangelists in red shirts
whip up fervour by the waves
and fail to see the baptism to come.

Fat drops nudge.

The group around the ice-cream booth
hovers like wasps for 99s.
Nobody leaves for cars
parked by the 40 minutes sign.

It falls so fast you see silver.
Jeans stick to legs, a too-tight skin
of crinkled denim. Five people
dive into a beach tent.
Others, who walk little these days,
sprint. A woman tilts her head
to drink unchlorinated water,
lets it run down her.

Summer

I went to find summer
and it was wave on wave
of ox-eyed daisies
behind a fence
at Penysarn.

It was children
on a path
behind coast bungalows
where tall grasses trap the heat.

It was a station
where I wandered down a platform
carrying youth
like an overfull glass.

I went to find summer.
It played near wild flowers,
fled down the long sands
to stand at a distance,
then hid away.

Winter

Intense tiger irises,
dark-brooked ice filigree,
glitter as she trails
diamante black velvet
over her shoulder
and prowls, eyeing distance,
down the year's catwalk.

The Snow Cat

Stale air hangs in the room,
begins to curl
like dying petals.

Illness,
but today we're going out.

I grasp your arm
afraid to break another bone,
to slip or skid
on steel ice.

Chatting about impassable mountain passes,
we buy bananas, apples, grapes
and daffodils, two opening.

We walk away
through the surprise of snow
falling,
touching our hair and sleeves.

On the sea front,
before the hills,
children have built
a snow cat.

Bleeding the Radiator

Somewhere I heard the wind is silent
until it meets objects, gets squeezed through channels.
Then it wails, whistles, makes music
with drainpipes. Today it rides
in slow sea rhythms, left-hooks the fir tree.
Steady as a ship's engine, my computer thrums.

On the stairs that creak and settle
I hear your footsteps, your measured pace
across the landing, then metal on metal,
air hissing like an opened can of cola,
silence. Our voices break it,
talking of ordinary things as if
playing a familiar game of cards
with no surprises. Your steps retreat. The wind halts,
then rolls again across the garden.

Relativity

At night, the moon,
hung like a Chinese lantern
in the dark tree of sky,
stirs questions in a life
of short distances.

But we have sent a rocket
far beyond it,
with words of peace
from a warring world,
and thirty years on
it's left the neighbourhood block
to carry our hope
into the void.

Catching the Connection

Twilight. Platform at Crewe.
A space among eddies of people,
enough for a man,
alone in a sea of Christian culture,
to stop and say to everyone, to no one,
It isn't fair, this hatred of Islam.

I stop like a wave
reaching an unexpected shore.
We talk of politics
but our eyes say human, *salaam.*

A rush-hour tide starts to part us
but his smile stays with me.
I carry it on the train for Bangor,
into the hills, along the coast,
a candle in the growing darkness.

rain on the roof—
after the semiquavers,
one bar's silence

Shadow World

for Mark and Maureen

On the white wall, a black horse:
you put up your thumbs to make its ears
and you can turn your hand into a rabbit,
dog, billy-goat, goose — look!

My grandson laughs, wants to learn the trick.
He's forgotten the rattling ghost at the door
for animals in magic lamplight.

Season of skeletal trees against silver skies,
darkening early, we press our noses
against frosty glass, look up at night,
see a reversal: on a black screen, white stars.

Between waking and sleep

Fell into a junk yard
of nations and flags,
turned a corner into waves breaking.
Sigh, bring tears, buckets and spades
for a dead grandfather
buying mints for the kiddies
in a Moelfre sweet shop.

If only we could fly into azure
where God's a far-out jazz musician.
If only we could rainbow all our lives
and sing as the sun falls
and scents are stronger—
the bluebell woods and the salt on your arm
and the oranges in the Austin Seven.

If only we could hold all people
and no one slipped down under carnations
and chiselled words, windblown
on the island with the church,
its granite and its stained glass saints
and hymns damp against the walls—

and always the sea's soft brogue,
never the headstones under yew,
just running through a summer's day of sand
with the blue silk air about you.

At Llaneilian

January: we searched for ancestors,
walked to a gate set in rain-darkened walls,
when the weathervane span like a propeller
and the church flew up over the sea,
carrying off Glad Jones,
late of this parish,
all of her neighbours
and even a robin on a nearby bush.
It rained so hard the streets were awash,
the cars aquaplaning,
but next day, the ground was covered
in snowdrops.

                    *

As we rose towards blue
I could see them below us.
One looked surprised.
Another puzzled over
the electric-into-soup
origins of life,
the history of *homo sapiens*.
The third was so dismayed
I shouted out
lemon zest,
waves breaking,
waterfalls –
oh, blue planet.

A voice out of the next grave said,
Oh, bacon butties. Oh, chips!

                    *

We've always told tales of an afterlife—
pennies for Charon, a cross round the neck.

We're just clever apes who lost
most of our hair in a lake.

We're recycled, at least:
I'd like spring flowers upon my grave
and a rowan tree, but we're so many
they need to plant us three deep.

*

out of the black earth,
in a bleak season of sleet,
snowdrops

*

Under the light of a Tokyo room,
the corners in shadow,
a young woman picks up
a cup of green tea –
the arm with fine down
so live in that moment—
and an old man says,
*I don't want
to become junk.*

I don't want to be
flesh gnawed by rats
dreamless
dog bones
slops
ash swept out of a grate.

We are wheat and waves,
hills and laughter,
and wouldn't you want
to stretch out your arms
in a wild blessing?

*

Last night, I thought I heard
the peal of bells above the clouds.
Firecracker dragon danced
to thunder drums
scattering daffodils over the land.

Momiji

Passion grows stronger in the old.
There is no November of the heart,
no leafless tree, no loveless cold.

This is the country of the bold,
the scarlet-hatted, pressing 'Start,'
as leaves in Fall flare red and gold.

This is a time of clearer sight,
of pruning out, remaking charts
not on a shrinking scale but grand,
when roses, running, waves and light
brighten against the borderland.